SMART
SPENDING

The Teens' Guide to Cash, Credit, and Life's Costs

by KARA McGUIRE

COMPASS POINT BOOKS
a capstone imprint

Compass Point Books are published by Capstone,
1710 Roe Crest Drive, North Mankato, Minnesota 56003
www.capstonepub.com

Editorial Credits
Angie Kaelberer and Catherine Neitge, editors; Ted Williams, designer;
Eric Gohl, media researcher; Laura Manthe, production specialist

Image Credits
Capstone: 36–37; Glow Images: Corbis/Tom Stewart, 20–21; Newscom: EPA/
Felix Kaestle, 28–29; Shutterstock: Aaron Amat, 41, auremar, 49, Catherine
Lall, 45, Cheryl Savan, 30, Creativa, 26, 50, cvalle, 48, Goodluz, 7, hxdbzxy,
56–57, iodrakon, 1, iQoncept, 14, 40, Jag_cz, 38–39, Karen Roach, 52–53,
mangostock, 10–11, Marie C Fields, 22–23, michaeljung, 9, 33, 54, 58–59,
Monkey Business Images, 42–43, monticello, 12, ollyy, cover, Pressmaster, 13,
Sergey Furtaev, 19, Stuart Jenner, 47, Syda Productions, 35, Valua Vitaly, 25;
SuperStock: Cusp, 4–5; Wikipedia: Public Domain, 31

Design Elements: Shutterstock

Library of Congress Cataloging-in-Publication Data
McGuire, Kara.
  Smart spending: the teens' guide to cash, credit, and life's costs / by Kara
McGuire.
    pages cm.—(Compass point books. Financial literacy)
    Includes bibliographical references and index.
    ISBN 978-0-7565-4923-7 (library binding)
    ISBN 978-0-7565-4932-9 (paperback)
    ISBN 978-0-7565-4940-4 (eBook PDF)
1. Finance, Personal—Juvenile literature. 2. Consumer credit—Juvenile
literature. 3. Teenagers—Finance, Personal—Juvenile literature. I. Title.
  HG179.M38327 2015
  332.02400835—dc23   2014003726

Printed in Canada.
032014   008086FRF14

TABLE OF CONTENTS

WHAT SHOULD I BUY?

We're confronted with decisions on how to spend our money every day. Some of the decisions seem small and unimportant. Should I buy flavored water or a soda? See a movie or buy a new video game?

Those small spending decisions add up to a lot of money over time and can make it difficult to afford bigger, more important purchases. Decisions about how we spend our money today also affect whether we'll have enough money to spend in the future.

Learning to make smart spending choices of all sizes is a critical life skill. So is choosing the right way to pay for purchases and how to be a savvy borrower.

CHAPTER ONE

SPENDING SMART

Money is a finite resource. There's only so much money available, and you have to make tough decisions about where your money goes. A good way to start is by understanding the difference between a need and a want. A need is an essential, a basic of life. Think food, water, shelter, electricity, and clothing.

Wants are items that are nice to have. Perhaps a tablet, a trip to the beach, new earrings, or an online subscription. Another term for wants is discretionary spending.

Sometimes there's a blurry line between needs and wants. Imagine you just got a new job. The office isn't within biking distance, and public transportation doesn't go in that direction. You will need a car to get to work. But what kind of car? You could look for an affordable used car that gets great gas mileage and is inexpensive to maintain. But it might not impress your friends. Or you could buy a more expensive new car that costs more to maintain, but it is exactly what you want. See? A car is a need, but the type of car you buy can veer into the want lane. This goes for clothing as well. You need jeans, sneakers, and T-shirts, but you don't need brand-name jeans, sneakers, or T-shirts.

Similarly, not everyone is going to have the same list of needs and wants. Some people will have items on their "need" list that are considered wants for others.

When you spend money, you give up the opportunity to do something else with it, such as save it or give it away. This is known as opportunity cost.

WANTS VS. NEEDS

How would you rate things in your own life? Is each one a need or a want?

Item	Want	Need
Cell phone		
Car		
TV		
Smartphone		
Water		
House or apartment		
Energy drink		
Sneakers		
Exercise equipment		
Bed		
Microwave		

WHAT'S MY NET WORTH?

Net worth is the amount left when you subtract what you owe from what you own. What you own are your assets. What you owe are your liabilities. It's normal for teens and 20-somethings to have a low or even negative net worth, because debt for college, housing, or cars takes a bite out of whatever savings they might have.

PERSONAL NET WORTH WORKSHEET

Assets	Value
Checking accounts	$
Savings accounts	$
Money market accounts	$
Savings bonds	$
Certificates of deposit	$
401(k)	$
IRA	$
Roth IRA	$
Smartphone/computer/electronics	$
Car/bicycle/scooter	$
Home furnishings	$
Jewelry, art, collectibles	$
Total Assets	$

Liabilities	Amount Owed
Credit card balances	$
Estimated income tax owed	$
Other outstanding bills	$
Car loan	$
Student loans	$
Other long-term debt	$
Total Liabilities	$
NET WORTH (Assets minus Liabilities)	$

Another choice for spending your money is donating it to a charity. Americans give about $300 billion per year to charity. We give to feel good, support causes we feel connected to, and make the world a better place.

One incentive for adults to donate to charity is the tax break they receive for that donation, provided they itemize their tax deductions. This doesn't always apply to teens or young adults, but it's something to explore if you give a lot of money or goods to charity.

The United States has more than 1 million charities. Deciding how much to give and which organizations deserve your money is not an easy task. You can check with your local Better Business Bureau or visit websites that rate charities' financial and ethical performance, such as Charitynavigator.org, Guidestar.org, or Smartgivers.org.

Money is just one way to support a cause. If you're short on funds, consider giving your time instead. Teens in Kansas City can join the Greater Kansas City Community Foundation's Teen Giving Institute. They meet monthly to do hands-on work and learn about evaluating a charity for potential grants or funds. Do some research to see if there's a similar group in your area. Churches and school organizations regularly do volunteer work as well.

Another idea is to ask family and friends to donate money to a charity you support instead of giving you birthday or holiday gifts. Also, some of your stuff might be useful to charities. For example, animal rescue organizations can use old towels, child welfare organizations might like gently used toys, and charity-owned thrift stores could sell your cast-off clothing. If you have the ability and the desire to help, be creative, ask about needs in your area, and be willing to share your time and your strengths.

Ask yourself: Is this a need or a want? If it's a want, wait a little. Don't buy something the moment you see it. Think it over for a day or two. If you still want it, then make the trip to purchase it. Absence often eliminates desire.

Research before you buy. Make sure you are getting a good price for an item by doing some research before you make the purchase. Before the Internet you'd have to go from store to store or make phone calls to check prices and other product details. Today it's much easier to compare prices, on the Internet or by using a barcode reader price comparison app in stores. But price isn't the only important factor. It's smart to also evaluate the store's return policy and do research on the quality of the product. You may be better off spending a bit more for a higher quality product or one that comes with guarantees.

Look for ways to reduce costs. Do you get a discount for paying cash? Have you searched for a coupon? Is there a discount for buying in bulk? Will the price go down if you wait? It can be time-consuming, but asking for a way to save money is not being cheap. It's being frugal.

EMOTIONAL SPENDING

Money isn't just about numbers on a page or bills in a wallet. Emotion, desire, and others' opinions play a part in the financial decisions people make. For example, you might buy an expensive pair of shoes on impulse because you want to show them off to friends at a big party.

Scientists and economists who study money behavior work in the field of behavioral economics. This field has grown in importance in recent years.

How should people approach money knowing that emotions and irrational decisions can get in the way?

1. Awareness is a good first step.

2. Always step back or think twice before making big money decisions.

3. Create a spending plan and stick with it.

Daniel Kahneman, PhD, who won the Nobel Prize for economics in 2002 for his work with behavioral economics, has some advice: "Slow down, sleep on it, and ask your most brutal and least empathetic close friends for their advice."

BUDGETING

A budget is a road map for your money to follow. Without a map, you can easily get lost or overshoot your destination. Similarly, without a budget, you can easily lose sight of your financial goals, pay your bills late, or overspend. Many Americans spend more than they make, which is how they accumulate debt.

Creating a budget can be as high-tech or low-tech as you want. Either way, the basic process is the same. The first thing to do is figure out how much income you have. Base this on your net pay—the money you actually get in your paycheck after taxes and other deductions are withheld. Next catalog your fixed expenses, which are costs that are always there and stay the same. Rent, car and insurance payments, and monthly subscriptions are examples of fixed expenses. Then track your variable expenses, which are the costs that fluctuate. For example, money for utility bills, food, and entertainment are considered variable expenses. They can be needs or wants, and we make choices about how much to spend. While food is certainly a need, whether to dine on an inexpensive tuna sandwich or a pricey tuna sushi roll is your choice.

Most experts suggest keeping track of your spending for a month or two to understand your variable expenses. You can do this by writing each thing you buy in a notebook, by using your debit card for all transactions and combing through your bank statements, or by using a free personal financial management app like Mint.com. Apps are easier to use with debit or credit cards because using them creates a record of what you spend.

If you're eager to get started, you can use past bank statements as a start and try to estimate the rest. But often we're not so great at estimating true spending behavior in our heads.

Once you have numbers for fixed expenses and variable expenses, subtract those amounts from your income. Do you come up with a negative number? That means you are spending more than you earn. You'll need to make some decisions about cutting costs or finding ways to earn more money. Spending less than you make is one of the most important money principles to know. If you keep fixed expenses low and spend less than you make, you will have more financial flexibility and freedom.

SAMPLE BUDGET FOR TEENS

Category	Monthly Budget	Actual Amount	Difference
INCOME:	Estimate Your Income	Your Actual Income	
Wages/Income Paycheck, Allowance, Birthday Money, etc.	$200	$210	$10
Interest Income From Savings Account	$5	$4	($1)
INCOME SUBTOTAL	$205	$214	$9
EXPENSES:	Estimate Your Expenses	Your Actual Expenses	
Savings			
Savings Account	$10	$10	$0
Bills			
Taxes—from Paycheck	$30	$32	($2)
Rent/Mortgage	$0	$0	$0
Utilities—Electricity, Cell Phone, etc.	$30	$30	$0
Groceries/Snacks	$15	$12	$3
Car			
Car Payment	$0	$0	$0
Car Insurance	$0	$0	$0
Gasoline	$20	$25	($5)
Shopping			
Clothes	$40	$35	$5
Other Shopping	$10	$0	$10
Fun			
Entertainment— Movies, Video Games, Pizza, Bowling, etc.	$20	$25	($5)
Other Expenses	Ski Club: $10	Ski Club: $10	$0
EXPENSES SUBTOTAL	**$185**	**$179**	**$6**
NET INCOME	**$20**	**$35**	**$15**

Source: http://www.moneyandstuff.info/pdfs/SampleBudgetforTeens.pdf

Do you have money left over? This is a good place to be. But you're not finished!

The next step is to look at where your money has been going and ask yourself if you're using your money the way you want. Are you saving for important goals such as college or a car? Do you have enough savings in case you want to go on a school trip? If not, it's time to tweak your budget so your money reflects your goals and values.

Remember money is just a tool that helps you live the life you want. Your budget is a road map for getting there. No one gets a budget right the first time, and your budget will need to shift as your life changes.

During your budget building, it's likely that you thought about your life and what's important to you. This will come in handy for prioritizing your spending. For most of us, money runs out before all of our goals and dreams are met. This means we have to make decisions about what to do with our money first.

Here are some guidelines to follow

- **Pay yourself first.** Find a way to save a little bit of money, even if it's just a few dollars. Set this aside before you do anything else. Ideally, you'll have the resources to save for multiple goals—emergency savings, retirement, and fun stuff such as vacations, a car, or a new TV.

- **Take care of yourself next.** You need food, shelter, and medical care. Be mindful of what you spend because the costs vary wildly.

- **Fixed big-ticket expenses come next.** Rent, car payments, insurance, debt payments, and college bills fall into this category.

- **List wants.** They could include monthly subscriptions, movies, trips, and other items and experiences that make life fun. If money is tight, you shouldn't rank these expenses above your bills and future goals.

There are so many ways to pay for the purchases you make. Here's the rundown, including the pros and cons of each method.

CASH

PROS

- Accepted everywhere. Even some other countries accept U.S. dollars.

- Tangible. Some experts say people think more about cash purchases because they see the money leaving their hands and notice when it runs out.

- No worries about debt. You can't spend more cash than you have.

CONS

- To get cash, you must visit your bank or find an ATM. ATMs are nearly everywhere, but your bank might not have a machine located where you need to withdraw money. Using another bank's ATM often involves a fee, and your bank may also charge you a fee on top of that.

- Cash that's lost or stolen cannot be replaced.

Credit means using money you've borrowed from a bank to make purchases today, with the intention of paying back the bank at a specific time. Credit cards are essentially short-term loans.

PROS

- Instant gratification. and convenience. You don't have to wait to buy a good or service until you have the money.

- Tracking. Credit card statements provide a nice monthly record of how much you spend.

- Rewards. Some banks issue rewards when you use their credit cards to buy things. The rewards can be redeemed for items such as airline tickets, merchandise or gift cards, or cash back.

- Credit history. If you manage your credit card account well, the history will help qualify you for more favorable terms for mortgages and car loans.

CONS

- Too convenient. Credit makes it easy to overspend.

- Interest. Banks charge interest for borrowing money with credit cards, unless you pay it back within the grace period. This means you are ultimately paying more for the items you purchased, reducing the amount of money for buying other things or saving.

- Access. Not everyone has access to or qualifies for credit cards.

- Acceptance. Not all stores accept credit cards because store owners have to pay fees to credit card issuers.

- Teens who apply for a credit card may need a co-signer. A co-signer—an adult who agrees to have his or her name on the credit card account as well—is liable for any money owed if the primary borrower stops paying the debt.

DEBIT CARDS

A plastic payment card issued by your bank that lets you access the money in your account.

PROS

- Accepted nearly everywhere.

- Convenient. Debit cards offer the convenience of credit without worrying about racking up a big bill.

- Fast. No counting out change or scribbling a check.

- Easier to get than credit cards. Most bank accounts now come with debit cards.

- Good for tracking. Debit cards provide a record of what you spent, which makes budgeting easier.

CONS

- Fees. If you spend more than you have in your account, you could be charged expensive overdraft fees, unless you link your debit card to a credit card or other account that covers deficits.

- Fraud. Credit cards have more protection than debit cards in cases of liability and fraud. If you don't report your lost or misused debit card quickly, you could be liable for up to $500 of purchases you didn't make. Plus your money can be tied up during the investigation.

- Buying with debit cards doesn't help build your credit history.

- Rewards for using a debit card are rare in the current banking environment.

Bitcoin

There are many ways to pay for things. Cash, credit, even on your phone. But a new method of payment is very different from any of those because it's not based on the U.S. dollar or any other country's currency. It's called bitcoin and is a virtual online currency that can be used to buy goods and services at a limited but growing number of stores and websites. Two young girls in San Francisco even accept bitcoin at their cookie stand.

Powerful computers must "mine" for bitcoins by solving complex math problems, but you can also purchase the "cryptocurrency" on exchanges. Not everyone has heard of bitcoin, but the currency has grown in notoriety as the value has fluctuated greatly, and one bitcoin exchange claims to have lost hundreds of thousands of bitcoins.

PREPAID CARDS AND GIFT CARDS

These cards look and work much like debit cards, but they are purchased at a store with cash, credit, or a debit card. Some can only be used at certain stores. Others can be used anywhere and reloaded with funds when the money runs out.

PROS

- Convenience of plastic without the worries that come with credit cards or the need for a bank account.

- Available to anyone, regardless of his or her credit history.

- Good for managing a budget. You can carry a certain card for each kind of purchase to help keep your budget in check.

. . . .

CONS

- May have complex terms and conditions. Prepaid cards you can use anywhere are less regulated than debit and credit cards, so it's even more critical that you understand the rules involved. Gift cards for use at specific stores and restaurants have more consumer protections.

- Fees. Using some prepaid cards incurs fees for nearly everything, from checking your balance to loading new funds.

- Protection. Unlike money in the bank, prepaid cards aren't always covered by Federal Deposit Insurance Corporation (FDIC) insurance.

- Stores can go out of business before you use a gift card, making it difficult, if not impossible, to get your money back.

Trading goods or services with others is a way to get what you need or want without using money or credit.

PROS

- Easy on the bank account. You can get something without having to save.

- Easy on the Earth. Trading items you no longer have use for is better for the environment than throwing them away.

CONS

- No protection. If the other person doesn't fulfill his or her end of the bargain, or you find the items or service are misrepresented, there's little you can do.

- Limited options. It may not always be possible to barter what you have for what you need.

SAVING IS GOOD ENOUGH FOR A RAPPER

Bling. Mansions. Pricey cars. Think of the lifestyle portrayed by rap artists, and these images of luxury probably come to mind. Money—earning and spending loads of it—is a recurring theme in rap music. But a rap song that reached No. 1 on the Billboard top 100 chart in 2013 sends a different message. Macklemore and Lewis' "Thrift Shop" explores themes of buying second-hand and saving money, as Macklemore explains in this interview with MTV:

"Rappers talk about, oh I buy this and I buy that, and I spend this much money and I make it rain, and this type of champagne and painting the club, and this is the kind of record that's the exact opposite. It's the polar opposite of it. It's kind of standing for like let's save some money, let's keep some money away, let's spend as little as possible and look as fresh as possible at the same time."

Macklemore

BALANCING ACT

If you have a checking account with a traditional bank, odds are you received a checkbook when you opened your account. Odds are also good that you haven't thought about your checkbook since and might not even know where it is. With forms of payment such as debit and credit cards, many checkbooks have been relegated to the back of the desk drawer. Fewer businesses even accept checks these days.

So when you hear the phrase "balancing a checkbook," you might think it doesn't apply to you. But it's essentially the equivalent of online budgeting or account management. It means writing down what you've spent and subtracting it from the total in your account, so you don't spend more than you have. Balancing your checkbook also allows you to compare what the bank says you've deposited and spent with what you think you've done, just in case there are errors.

I'D LIKE TO GIVE THE WORLD A COUPON

Coupons are believed to date back to 1887 and the Coca-Cola Company. At the time Coke was relatively unknown, and the coupon entitled consumers to a free glass of the bubbly beverage at a soda fountain.

Coupons help consumers spend less on goods they want or need, freeing money to spend on other items or to save to reach financial goals. Nearly eight in 10 consumers say they use coupons regularly, according to coupon clearinghouse company NCH Marketing Services.

Coupons can save a lot of money. But if the item or service being discounted isn't something you really want or need, getting a good price doesn't make up for the fact that you've just spent money unnecessarily. Also be sure to read the fine print on the coupon. Most coupons have restrictions on the type or number of items you must buy.

Coca-Cola's coupon campaign in the late 1800s was a huge success.

THIS CARD ENTITLES YOU TO ONE GLASS OF

FREE **Coca-Cola** AT THE FOUNTAIN OF

TRADE MARK REGISTERED

ANY DISPENSER OF GENUINE COCA-COLA

CHAPTER TWO

BRILLIANT
BORROWING

If you're in need of cash, one option is to borrow it. But borrowing is a major decision. You don't want to end up taking on more debt than you can safely pay back.

You might have heard the term "financing." That means taking out a loan to purchase a big-ticket item, such as a car, house, or furniture. Young people also commonly borrow money to pay for college. And when you pay for purchases with a credit card, you are using the bank's money and agreeing to pay it back. If you buy a candy bar with a credit card, you are borrowing money to pay for it.

You have several options if you decide to get a loan. You can ask family or friends for a loan. You can borrow from a bank, either through a credit card or a bank loan. It tends to be easier to qualify for a credit card than for a bank loan. Since the Great Recession of 2007–2009, banks have stricter loan standards.

Peer-to-peer lending websites such as lendingclub.com and prosper.com are another option. These sites allow strangers to lend and borrow money from one another.

COSTS OF BORROWING

Banks lend money to make money. When you borrow from a bank, the bank charges you interest. You must pay the interest back along with the amount you originally borrowed, which is called the principal. However, if you borrow money from friends and family, they might not charge you interest.

Whether to borrow from family and friends can be a sensitive issue so it's important to devise a clear plan for how to pay it back or you risk straining your personal relationships.

When you borrow money for a house or car, the lender will usually require a down payment up front. It's calculated based on the total purchase price of the item. A typical down payment is 20 percent of the purchase price, but smaller and larger down payments also may be allowed.

At one time it was very easy to get a credit card. Companies even used to market credit cards on college campuses, offering students free T-shirts and other goodies in exchange for filling out a credit application. The widespread availability of credit got some teens and young adults in trouble. And stories about how credit contributed to the financial problems of the Great Recession have some consumers fearing credit cards.

But credit isn't all bad. It's a way to make purchases easily without having to carry a lot of cash. Credit creates a helpful record of your spending and is a good safety net if you need money in a crunch. But the terms and conditions of credit cards, which often are buried in fine print, must be understood so you don't spend more than you can afford to repay or rack up unexpected interest and fees.

A good rule is to use a credit card for just the purchases that you can afford to pay off within the grace period, which is the amount of time you have to pay your credit card bill before you are charged interest. Interest on credit cards is measured with an annual percentage rate (APR), which means interest expressed over a year-long period. The grace period usually is about a month, but check with your credit card company to be sure.

WOULD YOU LIKE A CREDIT CARD WITH YOUR T-SHIRT?

Credit card companies are restricted by law from marketing cards the way they used to. If you're younger than 21, you must prove you have the income to pay your bill or have a co-signer who is older than 21 who agrees to pay if you can't. Another way to build credit is to have a parent add you as an authorized user to his or her credit card account.

Most banks require a minimum monthly payment on credit card accounts. Minimum payments tend to be small—as little as 2 to 3 percent of your total balance. But don't be tempted to pay only the minimum. The less you pay on your bill, the more you'll end up paying in the long run. If, for example, you have $1,000 in debt at an APR of 18 percent and your minimum payment is 2 percent, you'll pay a total of $1,863—$863 in interest—and take eight years to pay off the bill. If you doubled the minimum, you'd pay the debt in three years and save $600 in interest. If you don't have the money to pay your credit card bill in full, pay off as much as possible to limit the amount of interest you're charged.

this card and each month you pay ...
Only the minimum payment
If you would like information about credit counseling services, refer to w
1-877-285-2108.
rtant Information
WHETHER YO
additional charges using
payment
You will pay off t.
this state

Credit card companies are now required by law to include a section on the minimum payment on cardholders' monthly statements. The section should include how long it will take to pay off the bill at the minimum monthly payment, as well as the total amount charged.

In addition to minimums, there are also maximums. Cards have a credit limit, which is the maximum amount you can have on your credit card account at one time. Keep in mind that banks can set credit limits pretty high. Limits are no indication that you should charge that amount of money or could even afford to pay off that much debt.

Interest is just one type of fee banks may charge for credit card use. There are late payment fees, fees for using the card at ATMs, and fees for transferring charges you have on one card to another. Some banks also charge an annual fee for cards. These cards typically come with travel rewards or other benefits. It's important to calculate whether it makes sense to pay an annual fee for a credit card. In most cases the answer will be no, especially if it's your first credit card or you carry a balance. Cards that give users rewards tend to have higher interest rates.

you may have to pay a late fee up to $35.
riod, you will pay more in interest and it will take you longer to pay of

Balance shown on about ...	And you will end up paying an estimated total of ...
oj.gov/ust/eo/bapcpa/ccde/cc app	$517

Perks in the *Fine* Print

The fine print of credit card agreements is riddled with legal terms and hidden fees. But it also may contain perks that people may overlook.

PRICEY PIZZAS

It's Friday night and you're out with friends. You decide to go out for pizza. You are trying to be a savvy spender, so you buy the pizza special —$2 off a large pepperoni. You charge the $15 cost to your credit card. Your friends give you cash for their share, so your true cost was just $5. But you end up spending the $10 on candy and chips at the convenience store.

Let's say this scenario plays out each Friday. After a year you find yourself with a $750 credit card bill and only enough money to pay $20 a month. If your credit card charges an interest rate of 18 percent, it will take five years to pay for those large pies, and you'll pay an extra $361 in interest. It's a calculation that can give you massive indigestion, especially when you think about how that money could have paid for a new smartphone or other big purchase.

Three key perks of some credit cards
- Fraud protection: If your card is used without your permission, the law states you are not liable for more than $50 of the charges. Many major banks have zero liability policies for lost or stolen cards.
- Extended warranties: Some banks add more time to the warranty for items purchased with the card.
- Purchase protection: If you buy an item that is stolen or breaks right away, your bank might pay to replace it.

Your credit score is kind of like a grade-point average for your money life. It's used by banks to decide whether to lend you money and at what interest rate. But landlords or insurance agents also look at it when deciding whether to rent you an apartment or to determine your car insurance costs. If your score is in the basement, you could lose out.

There are several credit scores on the market, but most lenders look at the FICO score, which is named for the score's creator, the Fair Isaac Corporation. The score ranges vary, but the higher the score, the better. Some credit card issuers provide a free peek at your credit score. If they don't, you can purchase a score for less than $20 at MyFico.com or estimate your score for free at creditkarma.com.

Your credit score is based on your credit report. This document is filled with your financial history—which accounts you have and how well you've managed them. You have the right to receive one free credit report from each of the three major credit bureaus every year through www.annualcreditreport.com. You should take advantage of that free report not only to check for mistakes, but also to check for identity theft or other types of fraud.

1. **Keep your balance low in relation to your available credit.**

Keeping your credit balance to 25 percent or below your available credit is a good general rule. But don't open credit accounts you don't intend to use just to improve this ratio.

2. **Pay your bills on time.**

3. **Make more than the minimum payment.**

4. **Don't open a lot of new accounts over a short period of time.**

Having many inquiries into your credit report and expanding your available credit too quickly may signal to creditors that you're on the brink of major financial problems.

5. **Review your credit report regularly and correct errors.**

You can easily get your credit report online. Visit www.annualcreditreport.com and follow the instructions for correcting credit report errors with the credit bureaus.

Source: http://whatsmyscore.org/facts/

If you're having trouble qualifying for a credit card because you have no history or a low credit score, a secured credit card is one option.

A secured credit card requires you to deposit money in an account before making purchases. An unsecured credit card doesn't require any money up front. The bank is placing faith in you to pay back the charges.

BUYING YOUR RIDE

For many teens, buying a car is their first major purchase. When you buy your first car, you'll need all of your financial literacy skills—assessing needs versus wants; researching a big purchase; budgeting for the car payment, gas, insurance, and maintenance; and using savings or getting financing. They are all important when it comes to selecting the right vehicle for the right price.

HELP WITH DEBT

Overdue debt won't go away. It can reduce your financial options and make it tough to meet financial goals. Help is available for people who get in trouble with credit. If that happens to you, your parents or guardians are your first resource. They can help you find a certified credit counselor who is a member of a respected group such as the National Foundation for Credit Counseling (NFCC.org).

If you don't get help, creditors will start by charging you fees. Eventually they will send your bill to their collections department or a collections agency. This will hurt your credit score. Part of your wages can be garnished, a legal procedure in which money is taken from your paycheck to cover the debt you still owe. Some people who have a large amount of debt might consider bankruptcy. Although bankruptcy can be a fresh start for your finances, it's not something to enter into lightly. It hurts your credit history and score for years to come, making it tough to borrow money. Filing for bankruptcy can make it more difficult to rent an apartment or find a job because landlords and employers may look at your credit history.

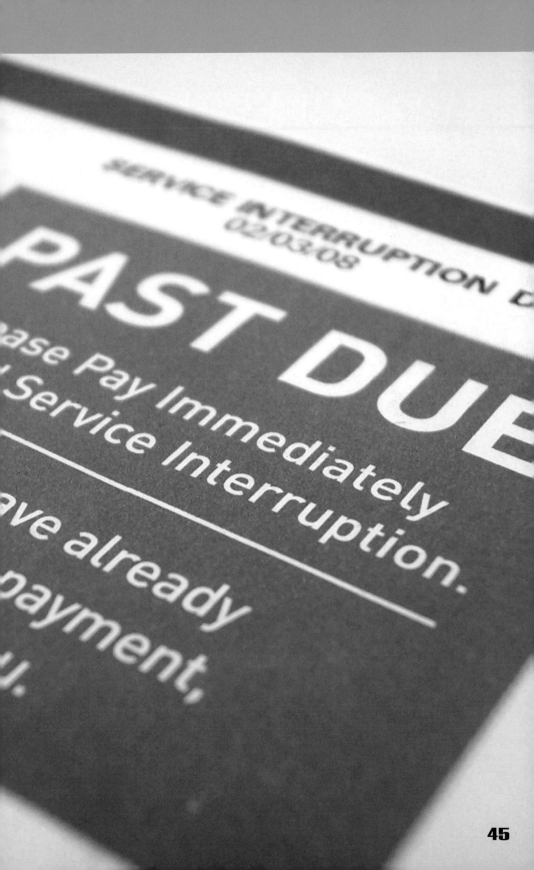

SERVICE INTERRUPTION D
02/03/08

PAST DUE

ase Pay Immediately
Service Interruption.

ave already
payment,

CHAPTER THREE

PAYING FOR COLLEGE

For many teens, college is the biggest expense of their lives so far. Fortunately, there is a lot of financial assistance available for getting that degree.

Most people can't afford to just pay for college. You would have to be quite wealthy to cover six figures' worth of college costs without blinking an eye. That's why it's important to understand all of the tools out there to help you.

Planning for college costs should start long before you head to campus. Some parents start saving before their kids are born! But even if you are in your last year of high school, it's better late than never. Online calculators can help you figure out your estimated family contribution for college, based on income and other factors.

When you are in high school, you and your family should fill out the Free Application for Federal Student Aid (FAFSA). This is the starting point for determining your eligibility for loans, work-study, and other programs created to help students pay for college. Fill it out even if you think your parents have too much money to receive aid.

What It Costs

$18,391. That's the average cost of a year's in-state tuition, fees, and room and board for a public college in 2013-14. The cost more than doubles for private schools. The main costs you should budget for include:

- Tuition and fees

- Room and board: The cost of your dorm room or apartment and cafeteria plan

- Books and supplies

- Spending money: The cost of things such as late-night pizzas, cell phone bills, clothes, and laundry. These costs vary, and many students are surprised by how quickly they add up.

- Transportation: The cost of your bus pass, bike, or car

Let's take a look at the main tools available to pay for college:

Savings: Money saved in a regular savings account or a 529 plan, which is an account dedicated to college costs.

Available cash: Money set aside from your or your parents' paycheck to cover college costs.

Financial aid: A broad term used to describe loans and grants given to a student from the school and the government to pay for college. Many types of financial aid are available from the federal government and private organizations. After you are accepted, your college will send you a financial aid letter detailing a proposal for how you'll pay for college. The most important thing to keep in mind is that financial aid is not necessarily free money. It often includes loans you must pay back. The key pieces of financial aid are grants, scholarships, and loans.

48

You're In!

Once you receive your college acceptances, it's time to decipher your financial aid award letters. Your high school guidance counselor should be able to help you, and you can find many resources on the Internet. The college's financial aid office can also answer your questions. As with any financial decision, you must understand every piece of a financial aid offer and how it compares with other offers you've received. You don't want any big dollar surprises as you set out on your own.

GRANTS AND SCHOLARSHIPS

Neither grants nor scholarships need to be paid back. Scholarships tend to be awarded based on merit, such as earning good grades, writing a great essay, or doing well in a particular activity. College, private organizations, and even your parents' employers may give scholarships. You can research many scholarships online. Just remember that legitimate scholarships do not require up-front fees. Your high school guidance counselor can help you find and apply for legitimate scholarships.

Grants tend to be awarded on the basis of financial need. Many college students receive Pell Grants from the federal government. Colleges give need-based aid as well, which allows some lower-income students to afford expensive private colleges.

LOANS

The federal government offers college loans. If you have financial need, you'll qualify for a subsidized loan   a loan that does not accumulate interest while you're in school. Other federal loans include unsubsidized loans, which do accumulate interest during your studies. The federal government also offers loans to parents called PLUS loans.

Banks also offer college loans, but be careful to read the fine print. These loans tend to have less favorable terms than government loans and often require a co-signer, such as your parent or guardian.

In addition, you can charge college expenses on a credit card. However, that isn't a recommended way to pay for college.

Researching and applying for college is filled with daydreaming, excitement, and possibility. Where will you go? What will you major in? What will your career be? A question that isn't always on that list but should be: How much can I afford to borrow?

It's a tough question to answer because there are so many unknowns about where college will take you and what career you'll ultimately have. But it's critical to explore some scenarios so you don't end up with crippling debt. College debt is nearly impossible to get rid of through bankruptcy. Debt forgiveness programs for federal loans don't start until you've been paying the debt for a decade or more in most cases. One strategy is to check out debt repayment calculators online, such as http://mappingyourfuture.org/paying/debtwizard. Or listen to an expert's opinion. "The total amount of student debt should not exceed the borrower's anticipated annual salary for the first year out of school," says Allesandra Lanza of the nonprofit organization American Student Assistance.

TIPS TO MINIMIZE
THE COST OF COLLEGE

1. Work part-time
2. Earn college credits in high school
3. Live at home
4. Buy used textbooks or rent your books
5. Graduate on time

Expert Advice on Saving for College

Kathy Ruby, a college finance consultant at getintocollege.com and a former financial aid director at St. Olaf College in Minnesota, has advice for would-be college students:

Talk to your parents or guardians.

Find out what they can afford and are willing to pay for your college education. It's not always an easy conversation (for them or for you), but it's one that you need to have.

Read your e-mail. Every day.

Colleges expect you to; it is how they will communicate with you about important things like required health forms, financial aid applications, and, of course, paying your bill. Unlike high school, colleges e-mail you, not your parents. Learn to manage your e-mail account: Sort e-mails you need to keep into folders, respond in a timely manner, and delete the ones you don't need. Unsubscribe yourself from advertiser mailing lists. In other words, avoid having 1,697 e-mails in your inbox.

Pay attention to deadlines.
They matter. Especially when it comes to getting money for college. Every college will have deadlines listed clearly on its Financial Aid Office website. And don't let the forms intimidate you. They are simpler than they look and can really pay off. Let's say it takes you three hours to complete the FAFSA, and, as a result, you are awarded a $3,000 grant. When was the last time you got paid $1,000 an hour, tax-free?

PUBLIC VS. PRIVATE

At first glance, public schools always look cheaper than private schools. But as with the sticker price on a car, most people don't pay the price you see listed in a college brochure. Because of scholarships, grants, and other awards based on financial need or performance, a private school may cost a student less out of pocket than a state school.

You can use a free online net price calculator to get an idea of the actual cost of attending a college. The federal government requires most colleges to include a version of this calculator on their websites.

HOW I'M PAYING FOR COLLEGE

Advice from a college student who is attending the University of Michigan with the help of scholarships and a lot of hard work:

Julia Goss, 19
Southgate, Michigan
Growing up in the suburbs of Detroit has put me close to the economic recession of the past decade. Attempting to pay for college on a minimum-wage budget has taught me to appreciate my hard-earned money. My three biggest money tips for teens and young adults, especially those planning to go to college, are:

1. Save before you spend.

2. When you want to buy something, resist the impulse and see if you still want it in a few days.

3. Remember that money is only a number and isn't the only definition of "success."

DO I REALLY NEED IT?

The next time you're tempted by all the glittering displays at the mall, you'll be able to decide if what you're seeing is a need or a want and handle it accordingly. You know what a credit score is and how important it is to maintain it. You can set up a budget for

yourself, and save for important purchases such as college, a car, and a home. You even can use some of the money left over to support the charitable causes you care about. You're well on your way to living a rich life—bling or no bling.

GLOSSARY

annual percentage rate (APR)—yearly interest rate charged on outstanding credit card balances

asset—item of value, such as money or property

behavioral economics—branch of economics that uses psychology to explain why and how people make financial decisions

budget—plan for spending and saving money

co-signer—person who takes on a joint obligation to pay back a debt; parents may be required to co-sign on loans to teens

credit score—number generated by a statistical model that is used to help financial institutions to decide whether to lend a consumer money; the higher the score, the better

down payment—money paid up front when making a major purchase involving borrowing; the down payment is typically calculated as a percentage of the total cost of the item

finance—to borrow money in order to buy something

fixed expense—an expense that stays basically the same from month to month, such as rent and car payments

frugal—careful in spending money and using resources

grace period—time a borrower is allowed after a payment is due to make the payment without additional interest being owed

interest—fee charged to borrow money; generally, interest is calculated as a percentage of the amount borrowed or lent

liability—something that is owed, such as loans and credit card debt

net worth—value of what you own after subtracting liabilities from assets

opportunity cost—next best alternative that is given up when a choice is made; for example, when you spend your money, you lose your "opportunity" to use it in other ways

variable expense—an expense that varies from month to month, such as food or clothing expenses

ADDITIONAL RESOURCES

FURTHER READING

Bissonnette, Zac. *Debt-Free U: How I Paid for an Outstanding College Education Without Loans, Scholarships, or Mooching off My Parents.* New York: Penguin/Portfolio, 2010.

Blumenthal, Karen. *The Wall Street Journal Guide to Starting Your Financial Life.* New York: Three Rivers Press, 2009.

Hansen, Mark. *Success 101 for Teens: Dollars and Sense for a Winning Financial Life.* St. Paul, Minn.: Paragon House, 2012.

Karchut, Wes, and Darby Karchut. *Money and Teens: Savvy Money Skills.* Colorado Springs, Colo.: Copper Square Studios, 2012.

INTERNET SITES

Use FactHound to find Internet sites related to this book. All of the sites on FactHound have been researched by our staff.

Here's all you do:

Visit *www.facthound.com*

Type in this code:
9780756549237

OTHER SITES TO EXPLORE

The College Board
https://www.collegeboard.org

The Mint
http://www.themint.org

Practical Money Skills for Life
http://www.practicalmoneyskills.com

SELECT BIBLIOGRAPHY

Bankrate. 6 May 2014.
http://www.bankrate.com

Board of Governors of the Federal
Reserve System. 6 May 2014.
http://www.federalreserve.gov

Charities Review Council. 6 May 2014.
http://www.smartgivers.org

Charity Navigator. 6 May 2014.
http://www.charitynavigator.org

The College Board. 6 May 2014.
https://www.collegeboard.org

Consumer Financial Protection Bureau.
6 May 2014.
http://www.consumerfinance.gov

Farrell, Chris. *The New Frugality.*
New York: Bloomsbury Press, 2010.

Federal Student Aid. 6 May 2014.
https://fafsa.ed.gov

Finaid. 6 May 2014. www.finaid.org

Guidestar. 6 May 2014.
http://www.guidestar.org

Mapping Your Future. 6 May 2014.
http://www.mappingyourfuture.org

The Mint: Fun Financial Literacy
Activities for Kids, Teens, Parents and
Teachers. 6 May 2014.
http://www.themint.org

National Center for Education Statistics.
6 May 2014. http://nces.ed.gov

NCH. 6 May 2014.
http://www.nchmarketing.com

Practical Money Skills for Life.
6 May 2014.
http://www.practicalmoneyskills.com

Projectionstudentdebt.org. 6 May 2014.
http://www.projectionstudentdebt.org

Robin, Vicki, and Joe Dominguez. *Your
Money or Your Life: 9 Steps to Transforming
Your Relationship with Money and
Achieving Financial Independence.*
New York: Penguin Books, 2008.

Schwab Moneywise. 6 May 2014.
http://www.schwabmoneywise.com/
public/moneywise/home

What's My Score. 6 May 2014. http://
whatsmyscore.org

SOURCE NOTES

Page 13, line 23: Jesse Singal. "Daniel
Kahneman's Gripe With Behavioral
Economics." *The Daily Beast.* 26 April
2013. 5 May 2014. http://www.
thedailybeast.com/articles/2013/04/26/
daniel-kahneman-s-gripe-with-
behavioral-economics.html.

Page 29, line 8: Natasha Chandel.
"Macklemore 'Pops Some Tags' While
Thrift Shopping." MTV. 20 Dec. 2012.
5 May 2014. http://www.mtv.com/
news/1699304/macklemore-thrift-shop/

Page 47, line 1: Trends in Higher
Education. https://trends.collegeboard.
org/college-pricing/figures-tables/
average-published-undergraduate-
charges-sector-2013-14. 14 May 2014.

Page 53, line 9: Christina Couch. "How
much college debt is too much?"
Bankrate.com. 5 May 2014. http://www.
bankrate.com/finance/college-finance/
how-much-college-debt-is-too-much-1.
aspx

Page 55, line 1: Phone and email
interviews. 7 Aug. 2013.

Page 56, line 14: Email interview.
18 Aug. 2013.

INDEX

About the Author

Kara McGuire is an award-winning personal finance writer, consumer researcher, and speaker. She writes a personal finance column for the Minneapolis *Star Tribune* and formerly worked for the public radio program *Marketplace Money*. She enjoys teaching young people and parents about money. Kara lives in St. Paul, Minnesota, with her husband, Matt, and children Charlotte, Teddy, and August.